Parker's Cars

50 YEARS OF THE BEST BLOOMIN' MOTORS
by Aaron Gold

An Hachette UK Company
www.hachette.co.uk

First published in Great Britain in 2015 by
Cassell, a division of Octopus Publishing Group Ltd
Carmelite House,
50 Victoria Embankment
London EC4Y 0DZ
www.octopusbooks.co.uk

ISBN 9781844038268

A CIP catalogue record for this book is available from the British Library

Printed and bound in China

10 9 8 7 6 5 4 3 2 1

"To Lady Penelope, who let
me drive the greatest
car h'ever conceived."

CONTENTS

INTRODUCTION

Not many people know this, but motoring is one of me passions in life. I've loved cars h'ever since I was a lad, and h'as soon as I was big enough to reach them pedals, I would ni… er, *borrow* me neighbour's motors and take 'em for a spin. Of course, working for M'Lady and H'International Rescue meant I got to drive one of the finest vehicles h'ever to grace the public roads, my beloved FAB 1. Two hundred mile h'an hour and no joke. That's Kent to London in less time than it takes to pop down to your local, barring any hassle from the rozzers. But 'ave you seen that traffic in London nowadays? The number of times I've been tempted to use them laser guns…

Oh, Lady Penelope is looking over me shoulder and telling me to get on with it. Yes, M'Lady.

FAB 1 has got me and Lady Penelope h'out of more tight situations than I care to remember, and I still think it's the greatest motor I'll ever drive. On the other hand, I've seen some flash jam jars come and go over the years, and there are plenty I wouldn't mind havin' a go in. (And more than a few I'd like to hand over to Brains for the FAB treatment.) So here, at M'Lady's request, are 50 of the finest motors I've ever seen, barrin' FAB 1. And a right good bunch they are too.

Parker

1965 ROLLS-ROYCE FAB 1

"I've driven some posh motors, but never h'anything as special as FAB 1. I loved that car h'almost as much as M'Lady herself."

Lady Penelope's bespoke Rolls-Royce is arguably the most exclusive vehicle ever produced by the world's most exclusive automaker. Little is known about the mechanical details, as they were kept confidential by Rolls-Royce at the request of Lady Penelope and Brains, who helped to develop the vehicle and its many armaments. FAB 1 was powered by a gas-turbine engine, presumably a heavily-modified unit sourced from Rolls-Royce's aero engine division, with power delivered to all six wheels through a proprietary gearbox. In keeping with Rolls tradition, power output was listed merely as 'Adequate for M'Lady.' FAB 1 was capable of speeds in excess of 200 mph on roads and up to 50 knots (58 mph) on water when the concealed hydroplanes were deployed to great effect.

The interior was designed for the comfort, convenience and protection of Lady Penelope, complete with Connolly leather upholstery, a full video communications system and a bulletproof Perspex canopy. Though the extent of FAB 1's armament is unknown, eyewitness accounts suggest that the car had front and rear machine guns, laser cannons, harpoon launchers, bulletproof tyres, a smoke-screen generator and an oil-slick dispenser.

FAB 1 was a one-off model designed exclusively for Lady Penelope. Unfortunately, it was stored in the cargo hold of *Skyship One* during its fateful maiden voyage and is presumed to have been destroyed in the subsequent crash and explosion. But a little thing like that would never get in the way of a Thunderbird mission.

CONFIDENTIAL
TOP SECRET
CONFIDENTIAL

SPECIFICATION

Manufacturer: **Rolls-Royce (UK)**
Production: **1965 (1 produced)**
Body style: **Six-wheel limousine**
Layout: **Front engine, all-wheel-drive**
Engine: **Classified**
Gearbox: **Classified**

1966 SHELBY COBRA SUPER SNAKE

Sidelined from his career as a racing driver and unwilling to go back to chicken farming in his native Texas, Carroll Shelby was looking to create the ultimate sports car. Years of racing in Europe sent him to America for his engines and Britain for everything else, and it wasn't long before he came up with the AC-Shelby Cobra, a happy marriage of the AC Cobra sports car and the Ford Windsor V8. Brilliant though it was, the 289 Cobra wasn't mental enough for Shelby, and he soon shoe-horned Ford's massive 7.0-litre V8 between the Cobra's aluminium fenders, creating a monster that could go from 0 to 100 mph and back in less than 14 seconds.

And yet that *still* wasn't enough for Shelby, so he set out to build 'the Cobra to end all Cobras'. Starting with a competition-spec 427 Cobra, he added twin Paxton superchargers which boosted the output to a staggering *800 horsepower*. He built just two of these Super Snakes, keeping one for himself and selling the other to Bill Cosby, who was so frightened by the car that he returned it soon after (it killed its new owner). The car was later immortalized in a sketch on Cosby's 1968 album, *200 mph*.

"Some of us don't want to return to our earlier careers, like Shelby here. Luckily, I get to use my safe-crackin' skills from time to time, but only on Lady Penelope's instructions. Shelby built a good-un 'ere though."

SPECIFICATION

Manufacturer: AC (UK)/Carroll Shelby (USA)

Production: 1966 (2 produced)

Class: Sports car

Body style: Two-door convertible

Layout: Front engine, rear-wheel-drive

Engine: 7.0-litre, twin-supercharged V8, 800 bhp

Gearbox: 3-speed automatic

1967 TOYOTA 2000 GT

Back in the 1960s, few petrolheads took Japanese cars seriously. They were underpowered and derivative, and their reputation for bulletproof build quality was still far in the future. That's why the 1967 Toyota 2000 GT came as such a shock. Here was a sports car that had it all: it was pretty, it was quick and it offered a driving experience that compared favourably with the Porsche 911 and Jaguar E-Type. Co-developed with Yamaha, the 2000 GT featured a lightweight aluminium body, four-wheel disc brakes, and a 150 bhp, 2-litre inline six, driving the rear wheels through a five-speed manual gearbox with a limited-slip differential.

Many Westerners got their first glimpse of the car in the 1967 film *You Only Live Twice*, in which Bond girl Aki speeds to 007's rescue in a 2000 GT (a convertible version specially constructed for the movie, reportedly because Sean Connery was too tall to fit into the coupé). Good as it was, the 2000 GT sold just 351 copies worldwide. Today it is one of the most collectible Japanese cars, with surviving examples trading for well over a million dollars.

"Stone the crows! If it's all right for Bond, it's all right for me."

1968 BIZZARRINI MANTA CONCEPT CAR

"Here's a car that looked to the future and h'influenced the industry for decades to come. Just like the Thunderbirds did."

In the mid-1960s, the established automotive designer Giorgetto Giugiaro wanted to cast out on his own and make a splash. He purchased a former Le Mans racer called a Bizzarrini P538, and from its bones created the Bizzarrini Manta, using his new 'folded paper' design language first seen on the 1967 De Tomaso Mangusta. The car made its debut at the 1968 Turin Motor Show, and suddenly Giugiaro's fledgling firm, Italdesign, was on the map.

Giugiaro called the Manta a 'one-box GT'. It had a steeply raked windscreen, no bonnet (not necessary as the engine was in the back), three-across seating with the driver in the centre, and a Corvette-sourced 5.4-litre V8 engine providing plenty of power.

If the Manta looks familiar, that's because it inspired a generation of supercars to come, including the Lamborghini Countach and the Italdesign-penned Lotus Esprit. And when Giugiaro brought the flat planes and sharp angles of the Manta to the Mk 1 Volkswagen Golf, it became the signature look of the 1970s. The Manta was a one-off that remains in private hands, but its influence was felt by the entire industry.

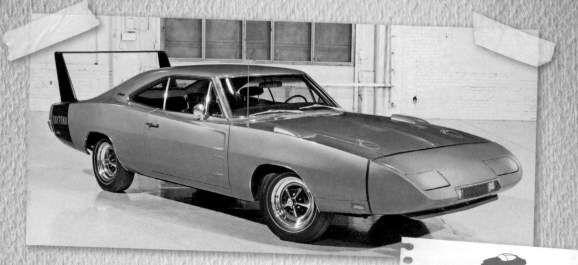

SPECIFICATION

Manufacturer: **Chrysler (USA)**
Production: **1969 (503 produced)**
Class: **Muscle car**
Body style: **Two-door coupé**
Layout: **Front engine, rear-wheel-drive**
Engine: **7.0-litre V8, 425 bhp or
7.4-litre V8, 375 bhp**
Gearbox: **4-speed manual or 3-speed
automatic**

1969 DODGE CHARGER DAYTONA

"The Yanks call this motor the 'Winged Warrior', which makes me think it's linin' up to be part of the Thunderbirds crew. Just needs a couple of wings."

In 1968, Chrysler's newly designed Dodge Charger was getting whipped in America's NASCAR races by Ford's fastback Torino and Mercury Cyclone. When the Charger's 'flying buttress' backlight was judged to be the problem, Dodge created the 1969 Charger 500 with a flush-mounted rear window and a blunt grille. Ford countered with the Torino Talladega and Cyclone Spoiler II, so the Dodge boys grafted on a pointy nose and a rear wing (mounted high enough to allow the boot lid to open, as NASCAR rules required racing cars to be production models) and the 1969 Charger Daytona was born. With a 7.0-litre Hemi V8 under the bonnet, the racing Daytona could reach 200 mph.

A Plymouth version called the Superbird followed in 1970. NASCAR had just changed its production requirements from 500 to one car for every two manufacturer's dealerships in the USA, which meant that Plymouth was forced to build nearly 2,000 street-legal Superbirds, while Dodge made just over 500 Charger Daytonas. The Superbird ended up being the better-known of the two cars, although differences in the sheet metal meant that the Daytona was actually slightly faster.

So successful were Chrysler's (and Ford's) 'aero cars' that NASCAR soon slapped them with a 5-litre (305 cubic inch) engine limit, which effectively rendered them non-competitive. Dodge continued to campaign Daytonas until 1971, when they were replaced with the newly designed, beakless and wingless 1971 Charger. Regarded as ugly and ungainly, street-legal Daytonas and Superbirds could be bought for a song in the early 1970s; today they are among the most collectible and valuable of Chrysler's muscle cars.

1970 CITROËN SM

When a French car gets it right, it gets it spectacularly right, and the Citroën SM is arguably the perfect example. Conceived as a sporty follow-on to the DS, the SM followed in the footsteps of The Goddess with its teardrop shape and self-levelling hydro-pneumatic suspension. Long, low, and exceptionally lovely, its crisp lines and angles above the beltline contrasted sharply with the voluptuous curves of the sheet metal below. The SM was a sensual beauty that showcased the best of early '70s European design.

To ensure they got the power-train right, Citroën bought Maserati — not just the engines, but the entire company. The Italian engine-maker supplied a modest 2.7-litre V6 developing 170 bhp (later increased to 3.0 litres and 180 bhp), and the SM could reach 140 mph; it cruised comfortably and confidently at 120 mph. It offered high-tech features that were decades ahead of their time, including variable-assisted power steering, headlights that turned with the front wheels and rain-sensing windscreen wipers.

Citroën sold nearly 5,000 SMs in 1971, but the SM's complicated engineering and laissez-faire attitude towards build-quality didn't endear it to buyers. Citroën declared bankruptcy and merged with Peugeot, which promptly sold Maserati and cancelled the SM. Citroën went on to find success with the mass-market GS and CX, and the SM went on to become a classic.

SPECIFICATION

Manufacturer: Citroën (France)
Production: 1970–75 (12,920 produced)
Class: Grand tourer
Body style: Two-door coupé
Layout: Front engine, front-wheel-drive
Engine: 2.7-litre V6, 170 bhp
Gearbox: 5-speed manual or 3-speed automatic

"I could say a lot of things about the French - some of 'em rude - but the Maserati-powered Citroën SM is an h'innovative motor and what M'Lady would call 'a timeless European classic'."

1971 DE TOMASO PANTERA

"This motor has got h'an American engine and an Italian soul – it's like a new-world, old-world couple who actually get along together. And fair do's, it would make a decent holiday car for Lady Penelope."

When it comes to cars, there are some things the Italians do well (like chassis that caress the road like an attentive lover) and some that the Americans do well (like big, noisy engines that have ridiculous amounts of power). In 1971, Argentinian racing car driver Alessandro de Tomaso sought to bring them together in the De Tomaso Pantera.

Key to the Pantera's success was Ford's involvement. Not only did they supply the 330 bhp, 5.8-litre V8 engine, but they also agreed to distribute the car in the USA. Styled by American designer Tom Tjaarda, the Pantera had the proportions of a proper Italian supercar, while its steering and suspension reflected De Tomaso's Formula 1 experience (which, admittedly, was less than successful). Performance was comparable to contemporary Ferraris and Lamborghinis: 0–60 in 5.5 seconds, 159 mph top speed – and yet the Pantera's price tag was less than half of other Italian exotics, with standard-fit air conditioning and the unmistakable rumble of an American V8 thrown in for free. Unfortunately, the Pantera's fit and finish were terrible and both the engine and the cabin were prone to overheating. Elvis Presley once shot his Pantera when it wouldn't start (the car is at the Petersen Automotive Museum in Los Angeles, with the bullet holes still in it).

SPECIFICATION

Manufacturer: **De Tomaso (Italy)**

Production: **1971–93 (7,260 produced)**

Class: **Sports car**

Body style: **Two-door coupé**

Layout: **Mid-engine, rear-wheel-drive**

Engine: **5.8-litre V8, 330 bhp**

Gearbox: **5-speed manual**

"With the Stratos, Lancia worked out that purpose-built machines work best. I could have told them that – hadn't they seen me beloved FAB 1?"

1972 LANCIA STRATOS

The Lancia Stratos was never intended to be a street car; its primary purpose was to take over from the Fulvia and ensure Lancia's continued success in rallying. Styled by Bertone's Marcello Gandini, it was as beautiful as it was functional: its wrap-around windscreen and pencil-thin A-pillars gave the car a familial resemblance to the Gandini-designed Lamborghini Miura. The engine, a Ferrari-sourced 2.4-litre V6 originally developed for the Dino 246 GT, produced 190 horsepower in street tune, giving the Stratos a 140 mph top speed. Racing engines started at 240 bhp and were turbocharged to over 550 bhp.

Lancia began racing the Stratos in prototype form in 1972, with the car scoring its first victory in Spain in 1973. Street-car production began that year, though a reduction in the production requirement meant that Lancia was able to wrap up Stratos production after building just 492 cars.

The Stratos accomplished its original mission, taking the World Rally Championship three years in a row (1974, '75 and '76), in a streak that ended prematurely when parent company Fiat decided to make the 131 Abarth the official factory-backed rally car. (The 131 picked up where the Stratos left off, winning the WRC in 1977, 1978 and 1980.) But the Stratos continued its strong showing, winning the Monte Carlo Rally in 1975, '76, '77 and '79, scoring its last major win at the 1981 Tour de Corse.

SPECIFICATION

Manufacturer: Lancia (Italy)

Production: 1973–75 (492 produced)

Class: Homologated rally car

Body style: Two-door coupé

Layout: Mid-engine, rear-wheel-drive

Engine: 2.4-litre V6, 190 bhp

Gearbox: 5-speed manual

1973 CATERHAM SUPER 7

There must be something in human nature that encourages us to take perfectly good ideas and mess them up. Caterham, bless their little corporate hearts, is one of the few companies that seem to know when and how to leave a good thing alone.

The original Lotus Seven was designed in 1957; it was a minimalist vehicle that embodied founder Colin Chapman's philosophy of making cars as simple and light as possible. 'Adding power makes you faster on the straights,' he famously said. 'Subtracting weight makes you faster everywhere.' Sold in kit form to dodge British purchase taxes, the Seven employed the minimum amount of hardware required to unite engine, gearbox, wheels and seats and make them road-legal and track-ready.

When Lotus discontinued the Seven in order to concentrate on more substantial cars like the Elite and Eclat, the rights and tooling were bought by Caterham Cars, a Lotus dealer named after its home town. In 1973 they introduced the Super 7.

SPECIFICATION

Manufacturer: Caterham (UK)

Production: 1973– present

Class: Sports car

Body style: Two-door cabriolet

Layout: Front engine, rear-wheel-drive

Engine: Various Lotus, Vauxhall, Ford, Cosworth and Rover engines

Lotus Cars were not immune to change, and the original Seven was updated several times over its 15-year production run; likewise, Caterham has continued to make subtle improvements to the Super 7. Today they sell four variants, ranging from the 140 bhp Seven 280 to the 310 bhp supercharged Seven 620 R (how does 0–60 in 2.8 seconds grab you?). And yet the essence of the car remains completely intact.

"For a solo mission, you'd be hard pushed to find many motors finer than this. Lady Penelope could'a done with a Caterham when she were evading them monorail crooks and me old mate Harry Malloy was pretending to be Grafton's driver. (A crook as a chauffeur? Unbelievable.)"

21

1974 LAMBORGHINI COUNTACH

"The Countach is h'an enduring classic that is as h'impressive today as it was when it was new. Classic, impressive, enduring – that's Thunderbirds, ain't it?"

The Lamborghini Countach may well be the ultimate supercar; at the very least, it's the vehicle that transformed Italian exotics from playthings of the wealthy into the dreams of the commoner on the street. Designed by Bertone's Marcello Gandini, the original Countach LP 400 was both subtle and extreme, a pyramidic design with a broad, flat windscreen and cool-as-hell scissors-style doors. Though the trademark scoops were in place (necessary to keep the V12 engine cool), the Countach had yet to sprout the fender flares, air dams and V-shaped rear spoiler that would give the car its signature look. Those would come on the 1978 LP 400S, along with the trademark phone-dial wheels wrapped with mile-wide Pirelli tyres.

Performance numbers for the original 4.0-litre, 375 bhp LP 400 are a subject of debate: Lambo claimed a 0–100 km/h (62 mph) time of 5.2 seconds and a top speed of 186 mph though contemporary reports were as pessimistic as 6.8 seconds and 170 mph. But the Countach had captured the hearts, minds and posters of petrolheads worldwide, and Lambo continued to improve it. By 1985 the 5000QV (quattrovalvole) was up to 5.2 litres, 4 valves per cylinder and 455 bhp, with its 0–60 time down to 5 seconds and a top speed over 180. It was enough for the 10-year-old design to keep up with the much newer Ferrari Testarossa. Throughout its 16-year production run, the Countach was the standard by which supercars were judged, and its performance and styling are impressive even by today's standards. Not bad for a design that stretches back over 40 years.

SPECIFICATION

Manufacturer: Lamborghini (Italy)
Production: 1974–90 (2,049 produced)
Class: Sports car
Body style: Two-door coupé
Layout: Mid engine, rear-wheel-drive
Engine: 4.0-litre V12, 375 bhp
Gearbox: 5-speed manual

1975 PORSCHE 911 TURBO

Like several cars in this book, the 911 Turbo was developed in the interest of homologation (getting a certificate to race). In order to qualify the 934 for FIA Group 4 racing, Porsche needed a street-legal version. Known internally as the 930 – and externally as the 911 Turbo – the road car was so successful that it soon became an end rather than a means.

A single turbocharger boosted the 3-litre, flat-six engine to 260 bhp, 60 more than the normally aspirated engine fitted to the Carrera 3.0. The existing 5-speed gearbox couldn't handle the additional torque, so Porsche fitted a 4-speed, much to the chagrin of many buyers. (The 911 Turbo wouldn't get a fifth gear until 1988.) Even with only four cogs, performance was unreal by the standards of the day: 0–60 in just over 5 seconds and a top speed of over 150 mph.

The 911's handling was already known to be tricky, so Porsche upgraded the suspension, widening the front track by 7.6 cm (3 in) and the rear track by 15 cm (6 in). With the fenders flared around the outrageously wide tyres and a big 'whale tail' spoiler on the engine cover, the 911 Turbo's iconic look was born, and posters of the 911 Turbo began vying with Lamborghini for wall space. Production continues to this day, but the original remains the best.

Manufacturer: Porsche (Germany)
Production: 1980–89 (21,589 produced)
Class: Sports car
Body style: Two-door coupé
Layout: Rear engine, rear-wheel-drive
Engine: 3.0-litre turbocharged, horizontally-opposed six, 260 bhp
Gearbox: 4- or 5-speed manual

"The spoiler on this ain't nothin' compared to someone telling the end of one of my stories before I get there meself. There's nothin' like a pint down the pub with me mates and a rollickin' good FAB 1 tale to tell."

1976 ROVER SD1

"They called this 'a poor man's Aston'. Poor man, my life! At over 14 grand, this weren't no snip, but I remember it were dead flash and I could'a done with one in the mansion garage."

SPECIFICATION

Manufacturer: British Leyland (UK)

Production: 1976–86 (303,345 produced)

Class: Executive car

Body style: Four-door hatchback

Layout: Front engine, rear-wheel-drive

Engine: 3.5-litre V8, 155 bhp

Gearbox: 5-speed manual or 3-speed automatic

With fastback styling inspired by the Ferrari Daytona and an all-aluminium V8 under the hood, the Rover SD1 was the long-awaited replacement for the well-respected P6. It was an instant hit with both pundits and the public. Despite having several factors working against it – including an interminably long gestation period, a cabin in need of class and woeful budget constraints – the SD1 (or 3500, as the first model was known) won the European Car of the Year award in 1977.

The first 3500s offered 155 horsepower from the Buick-sourced 3.5-litre V8, providing a top speed just shy of 125 mph. Four- and six-cylinder versions followed, but ultimately the SD1 to have was the Vitesse, introduced late in 1982. Its 190 bhp fuel-injected version of the 3.5 moved it from 0–60 in 7.1 seconds and gave it a top speed of 135 mph. The chassis was optimized with a lowered suspension and bigger wheels and brakes. Naturally, the SD1 enjoyed all of the issues that typically plagued British Leyland cars: lousy build quality, iffy electrics and sporadic labour unrest. But the design was solid, and many regard it as the last 'real' Rover, as the brand would spend the next 20 years selling thinly disguised Hondas. Fortunately, the SD1 was a high note on which to exit.

1977 AMC CONCEPT 80 AM VAN

"*I remember the shock on those Yanks' faces when they saw this little number. At the time they were all driving around in Chevy estates as long as the Queen's Daimler!*"

In the mid-1970s, when high petrol prices and emissions regulations killed the muscle-car business, Americans turned to custom vans with side exhaust pipes, deep-tinted windows and turbine-style wheels. But the AM Van wasn't just an attempt to pander to the shaggin'-wagon set: the American Motors Corporation (AMC) presented it as part of its 'Concept 80 program', a group of concept cars that demonstrated the ailing company's vision of motoring in the fuel-starved 1980s. It was presented as a future concept, powered by a fuel-efficient, turbocharged engine with four-wheel-drive (in reality it was a fibreglass styling mock-up with no power train).

The AM Van correctly predicted the rise of the MPV and the all-wheel-drive 'soft roader', as well as the compact turbo engines that are now becoming popular in mass-market cars.

Unfortunately, AMC was haemorrhaging money, and after a failed partnership with Renault, the company was bought by Chrysler and dissolved. Happily, the AM Van still exists in a private collection.

1978 BMW M1

In the late 1970s, BMW partnered with Lamborghini to build a mid-engine racing car. The racing plans fell through and Lamborghini dropped out due to their impending bankruptcy, but what emerged was a car unlike anything BMW (or anyone) has created before or since.

The M1 was styled by Giorgetto Giugiaro, which explains its resemblance to the Lotus Esprit. BMW's primary contribution, besides the twin-kidney grille, was the engine: a lovely 3.5-litre, 24-valve DOHC inline six (what else would you expect from BMW?) that produced 277 horsepower in street trim and up to 850 in turbocharged racing form. It did a bit of racing in 1979, primarily in a specially created (and short-lived) Procar series. The M1 proved to be a mediocre race car, but as a road car it was outstanding, with sparkling performance (0–60 in 5.5 seconds, 162 mph top speed) and that brilliant sense of feedback and control that BMW does so well. Just over 450 were made over a four-year production run, 60 of which were built to racing spec. It was a failed experiment that resulted in one of BMW's finest creations.

"This 'ere reminds me of a beautiful Italian woman who once caught me eye in Rome. A'course I were too busy to stop and chat, but I often wonder what would'a happened if we'd had a bit of time. Some of the good ones pass by too quick."

29

"The 5.0 V8 done a right good job rescuing the Ford Mustang's performance image. Meaning it made them look right good. Brains his'self could 'ardly have done a better job."

1979 FORD MUSTANG 5.0

inch Windsor V8, better known as the 5.0 – a number that has become synonymous with the Ford Mustang. (For those who like to know: the actual displacement in cubic centimetres makes it a 4.9-litre engine, not a 5.0.)

The 4.9-litre 5.0 was dropped one year later, but returned with a vengeance in 1982 in a 157 horsepower High Output ('HO') version. Just five years later (1985 for those not counting) the 5.0 HO engine was up to a credible 210 horsepower. A 1987 redesign with flush aerodynamic headlights (only just made legal in the USA) and a grille-free nose turned the Mustang into an attainable dream. Vanilla Ice was rollin' in his five-point-oh (with the ragtop down so his hair could blow), while state cops in New York and California were employing the 140 mph Mustang LX 5.0 to catch the scofflaws who could outrun their Dodge Diplomats and Ford Crown Victorias (see pages 52–53).

The 5.0 gave way to an overhead-cam 4.6-litre V8 for the 1996 model year, but an all-new 412-bhp, 5.0-litre V8 (one that actually displaced 5.0 litres) appeared in 2011. The 5.0 V8 continues to ensure the Mustang's place as a performance icon.

SPECIFICATION

Manufacturer: **Ford (USA)**
Production: **1979–95, 2011–present**
Class: **Pony car**
Body style: **Two-door coupé**
Layout: **Front engine, rear-wheel-drive**
Engine: **4.9-litre V8, 140 bhp**
Gearbox: **4-speed manual or 3-speed automatic**

Just as Ford woke up the motoring world with the original 1964½ Mustang, they put it right back to sleep with the 1974 Mustang II, an econobox that sold well but virtually erased the Mustang's performance image. The all-new 1979 Mustang showed that Ford had regained the plot, and top among the new engine offerings was a 302 cubic

1980 RENAULT 5 TURBO

Most racing series require cars to be based on production models, so that the cars we watch zooming about on the telly have at least some relationship to the cars we drive. Few automakers have stretched the boundaries like Renault did with the 5 Turbo, which they designed for victory in the World Rally Championship. Renault did make a road-legal R5 Turbo, and sure, it was exactly like an ordinary Renault 5… at least as far as the door handles go.

Opening the bonnet of a garden-variety R5 revealed a 45 horsepower, 1.1-litre engine driving the front wheels. Opening the bonnet of an R5 Turbo revealed little more than the steering gear, because the engine was behind the front seats – a 1.4-litre turbocharged screamer that put out 158 bhp in street form and up to 350 bhp in racing tune. The rear suspension borrowed heavily from the Alpine-Renault A310, with ridiculously wide fender flares to make room for ridiculously wide tires.

The racing version never did achieve its goals; it won Monte Carlo in 1981, but was soon outclassed by the new breed of

"The Renault Five Turbo weren't no ordinary R5 - just like FAB 1 weren't no ordinary Rolls-Royce. This was the business."

all-wheel-drive Group B cars. Still, the street-legal 5 Turbo was mental: 0–60 in under 7.5 seconds, a top speed of 125 mph and go-kart handling. A review in *Hemmings Motor News* read: 'The car almost turns on its axis, with that engine screaming inside the car with you. What a sensation! It's like a French hillbilly's weekend project gone wonderfully right.'

Manufacturer: **Renault (France)**
Production: **1980–85 (5,007 produced)**
Class: **Homologated rally car**
Body style: **Two-door hatchback**
Layout: **Mid-engine, rear-wheel-drive**
Engine: **1.4-litre turbocharged inline four, 158 bhp**
Gearbox: **5-speed manual**

1981 DELOREAN DMC-12

The DMC-12 was invented by John DeLorean, a character every bit as interesting as that of the car he created. One of General Motors' youngest executives, DeLorean's flashy demeanour put him in continuous conflict with the company's conservative management. But he was a proven winner: he turned the Pontiac brand from a pensioner's special into a performance icon, most notably by bending GM's engine-size rules to create the 1964 Pontiac GTO, and managed to bring the lumbering giant Chevrolet under financial control. A candidate for the company's presidency, DeLorean instead quit GM in 1973 and started his own firm.

SPECIFICATION

Manufacturer: **DeLorean (Northern Ireland/USA)**

Production: 1981–82 (8,583 produced)

Class: Sports car

Body style: Two-door coupé

Layout: Rear engine, rear-wheel-drive

Engine: 2.9-litre V6, 130 bhp

Gearbox: 5-speed manual or 3-speed automatic

The DMC-12 prototype was unveiled in 1976, but problems with the new manufacturing methods DeLorean had hoped to employ led to a complete redesign, largely by Lotus founder Colin Chapman. After numerous delays, the first production car finally rolled out of DeLorean's government-funded Northern Ireland plant in 1981. With its angular Giorgetto Giugiaro-styled body, gull-wing doors, and unpainted stainless-steel exterior, the DeLorean was a breathtaking sight that instantly caught the fancy of car enthusiasts, though performance from the 2.9 litre-Peugeot-Renault-Volvo V6 was underwhelming. Unfortunately, accumulated delays, poor assembly quality and a lack of actual buyers put the company onto rocky financial ground. John DeLorean was arrested on cocaine trafficking charges, claimed police entrapment and was acquitted, but the DeLorean Motor Company collapsed. The story might have ended there, had the car not been used as a time machine in the film *Back to the Future*. Instead, the DeLorean DMC-12 became an instant icon.

"DeLorean was a right interesting character. I reckon he would have had some tales to tell. M'Lady said he seemed a 'charming gentleman' when she met him in Monte Carlo."

"Sometimes you 'ave to make do with whatever you've got on yer - like I did when Lady Penelope and Sir Jeremy got stuck in that gas-filled cellar. Seemed only reasonable at the time to pull the bloomin' doors off."

1982 CHEVROLET CAMARO Z28

American car enthusiasts refer to the late 1970s and early '80s as the 'Malaise Era', a time of rampant motoring mediocrity with precious few bright spots. American carmakers were obsessed with the switch to smaller front-wheel-drive cars; in retrospect it seems a miracle that the Camaro was spared that indignity. Sticking with rear-wheel-drive meant the new third-generation Camaro had to make do with a solid rear axle and recirculating-ball steering, but it did get contemporary angular styling that would age well – which was fortunate, because GM did not redesign it for more than a decade.

The Z28 was the fastest Camaro on offer, and while straight-line performance wasn't amazing – a 165 bhp, fuel-injected V8 was the best Chevy could come up with – the chassis engineers did a credible job with the suspension, which was no mean feat, considering the ancient hardware that they had to grapple with. *Motor Trend* named the Z28 their 1982 Car of the Year, and *Car and Driver* called the 1983 version of the Z28 'the closest thing to a race car built on an American assembly line, closer even than the Corvette'.

The Z28 sold in massive numbers (selling over 100,000 in 1984 alone) before the name disappeared altogether in favour of the IROC-Z.

SPECIFICATION

Manufacturer: General Motors (USA)

Production: 1982–87 (436,017 produced)

Class: Sports car

Body style: Two-door coupé

Layout: Front engine, rear-wheel-drive

Engine: 5.0-litre V8, 165 bhp

Gearbox: 4-speed manual, or
   3-speed automatic

1983 FORD THUNDERBIRD TURBO COUPÉ

By the early 1980s, the once-sporty Thunderbird had morphed into the stereotypical Yank Tank: overstuffed, over-chromed and woefully underpowered. Americans looked longingly at the small, sporty cars sold across the Atlantic. And then one day, seemingly out of the blue – or perhaps we should say out of the Blue Oval – came the Ford Thunderbird Turbo Coupé.

The new T-Bird's trim dimensions and aerodynamic styling were certainly European-inspired, but what really stunned the motoring masses was the 2.4-litre, turbocharged four-cylinder engine under the bonnet, which drove the rear wheels through a five-speed manual gearbox. The engine's 155 horsepower provided enough power for an 8.4 second 0–60 run and a 140 mph top speed. Output was up to 190 bhp by 1987, and despite an unsophisticated suspension

(MacPherson struts up front, live axle out back), the Turbo Coupé could keep up with BMWs in the curves. Other US carmakers introduced their own 'Euro-style' cars with turbocharged engines, but nothing delivered quite the experience of the Turbo Coupé.

The Turbo Coupé would be replaced in 1989 by the Super Coupé, a bigger and more contemporary T-Bird with a supercharged V6 and an independent rear suspension. It was a more sophisticated car, but it never had the impact of the Turbo Coupé, which showed that American carmakers were capable of rising above mediocrity.

"It's a Thunderbird, ain't it? It's got a beauty of h'an engine, purrin' away in there. And it don't look like much on the street. That's a perfect getaway vehicle right there. Not that I'm lookin' for one, mind."

SPECIFICATION

Manufacturer: **Ford (USA)**
Production: **1983–88 (128,533 produced)**
Class: **Personal luxury**
Body style: **Two-door coupé**
Layout: **Front engine, rear-wheel-drive**
Engine: **2.4-litre turbocharged inline four,**
 155 bhp
Gearbox: **5-speed manual, 4-speed automatic**

1984 FERRARI TESTAROSSA

"The slats on this would'a been perfect for firing Ma's exploding beans that time me and Lady Penelope were gallivantin' with Jeremiah Tuttle near that mine. Course we saved the day, but this nice little cruiser would'a come in dead handy."

The Ferrari Testarossa arrived at the height of the high-rolling 1980s, just in time for the premiere of TV show *Miami Vice*. The two joined forces in 1986, when Crockett's fake Daytona was blown up and replaced by a genuine Testarossa. As a result, perhaps, this car earned pride of place on the poster-laden walls of countless pre-pubescent boys.

The Testarossa was a follow-on to the 512 Berlinetta Boxer; Ferrari carried over the 4.9-litre, 48-valve, 12-cylinder engine but moved the radiators to the rear to increase luggage space and make a cooler cabin. This explains the massive side strakes, which were controversial at the time but helped to make the Testarossa a supercar icon. And it was a proper supercar, with 390 horsepower, a 5.2-second 0–60 time and a top speed of 181 mph. Despite a supercar price, 7,177 copies were sold before Ferrari upgraded it to the 512 TR in 1991.

1985 BENTLEY TURBO R

As independent and vibrant as Bentley is today, it's easy to forget that the company spent decades in the shadow of Rolls-Royce, churning out Silver Shadow clones for people who apparently wanted everything a Roller offered but without quite so much prestige.

The Turbo R was the Bentley that dared to be different: big alloy wheels, a deep front air dam, and even – I say, old boy, such scandal! – a body-colour grille-surround instead of chrome. Under the bonnet was a turbocharged version of Bentley's 6.75-litre V8. In keeping with tradition, Bentley would not publish output, but with a kerb weight of about 2,400 kg (5,300 lb), a 0–60 time of under 7 seconds and a top speed of 135 mph, the low-revving V8 was guesstimated to be putting out around 300 bhp and 450 lb-ft of torque. The chassis was updated as well, with a stiffened suspension that delivered handling to match the Turbo R's acceleration. And while the performance may have been German, the cabin was purely British: hand-rubbed, burr-walnut veneer dashboard, Wilton wool carpets and sport-style seats covered in hand-stitched Connolly leather. This was, after all, a car built by and for civilized people.

"I've h'always been a Rolls-Royce man meself, but 'ere's a Bentley I'd be proud to 'ave as me own."

1986 FORD SIERRA RS COSWORTH

Ford thought they had a winner on their hands when they launched the futuristic Sierra in 1982, but British buyers were put off by the jelly-mould styling and the old-tech engines and gearboxes. Sierras languished on dealer forecourts while potential buyers sought out left-over Cortinas, Escorts or – even worse – Vauxhall Cavaliers. Ford desperately needed a hero, so they went to long-time partner Cosworth to help them create one.

Cosworth had worked up a 2.0-litre, 204 bhp version of Ford's T88 engine, and it was a natural fit for the uber-Sierra. The boy-racer looks sprung from functional aerodynamic improvements, with a big cutout in the grille to feed air to the intercooler, and a giant spoiler above the boot to kill the lift generated by the three-door hatchback body. Performance numbers were strong: 0–60 in 6.2 seconds and a top speed of 145 mph, enough to see off the significantly pricier BMW M3 and Mercedes 190E 2.3–16.

The Sierra Cosworth would go on to bigger and better things, including the 224 bhp RS500 and the four-door Sapphire RS Cosworth, which later gained four-wheel-drive and a 220 bhp engine. Most importantly, the 'Cossie' took the Sierra from oddity to desirability.

SPECIFICATION

Manufacturer: **Ford/Cosworth (Germany/UK)**

Production: **1986–92 (30,932 produced)**

Class: **Hot hatchback**

Body style: **Three-door hatchback**

Layout: **Front engine, rear-wheel-drive**

Engine: **2.0-litre turbocharged four-cylinder, 204 bhp**

Gearbox: **5-speed manual**

"The Sierra got off to a bad start, so Ford
sent in Cosworth to rescue their failing
reputation. Slap-up job they did of it too."

SPECIFICATION

Manufacturer: **General Motors (USA)**

Production: **1987 (547 produced)**

Class: **Sports car**

Body style: **Two-door coupé**

Layout: **Front engine, rear-wheel-drive**

Engine: **3.8-litre turbocharged V6, 276 bhp**

Gearbox: **4-speed automatic**

1987 BUICK GRAND NATIONAL GNX

In the early 1980s, the Buick Regal was an old-man's car that bore an uncannily close resemblance to a sofa: soft and comfortable but poorly suited to rapid forward motion. Hence the shock and awe in '84 when Buick introduced a sporty version called Regal Grand National, a blacked-out beauty with barely a hint of chrome on its flanks. Under the bonnet was Buick's turbocharged 3.8-litre V6, first introduced in 1978 with an unimpressive 165 bhp rating. With sequential fuel injection and a distributorless ignition (both firsts for an American car), it now produced a credible 200 horsepower, enough for a 0–60 run of 7.5 seconds.

By 1987 output was up to 245 bhp and the time from 0–60 was down to 6 seconds. But this was to be the last year for the Regal's ancient G-body platform, and Buick decided to give the Grand National a proper send-off with the limited-run GNX. A fortified turbocharger boosted output to 276 bhp (a figure widely regarded as an underestimate), while a beefed-up rear suspension helped the GNX get power to the ground. The Regal's handling was a lost cause; even with massive Goodyear Eagle Gatorback tyres, the

"M'Lady once said that if she lived in New York, the Buick would 'ave been the thing. Luckily, she lives in Kent and Bonga Bonga, saving me from the indignity of drivin' an American motor. Push come to shove, though, the Buick would be a nifty choice."

GNX could only manage 0.80 g of lateral grip. But man, was it ever quick: Buick claimed a 0–60 time of 5.5 seconds and several magazines timed it at less than 5. It's no surprise that the GNX is now among the most collectible American cars of the era and represents a bright spot in Buick's history.

1988 PONTIAC BANSHEE IV

"This looks like one of them fast cars The Hood would drive. He were always trying to match the Thunderbirds, but he was well out-a-luck. Though this one did have a few of them future tech things."

The late 1980s were heady times for Pontiac, as the brand regained the performance image it first had in the 1960s. 'We build excitement!' blared the adverts; indeed, Firebirds were once again getting potent engines under their bonnets. It was into this era that the Banshee IV arrived, the fourth (and final) in a series of concept cars foretelling the future of the Firebird and Trans Am. Big, bright and bold, the Banshee IV wasn't just a styling exercise; it was a functional car powered by a 4.0-litre overhead cam V8 that presaged GM's much-vaunted Northstar engines. The Banshee's interior showcased future technologies that would eventually become reality, including a head-up display, steering-wheel-mounted controls and a moving-map navigation system. The next-gen Firebird bore a strong resemblance to the Banshee, particularly the pointed prow and long, low windscreen. Though the 'Bird's lot would improve, other Pontiac models yielded to the corporate anonymity that plagued the rest of GM's American brands. Pontiac never recovered, and closed for good in 2010.

1989 ASTON MARTIN VIRAGE

The Virage was the first totally new Aston Martin since the mid-1960s (provided you forget the 1976 Lagonda, which many people would be happy to do). Its clean, understated styling took the basic shape of earlier Aston grand tourers like the DBS and updated it, but the real work of art was to be found under the bonnet. Aston brought their aging aluminium 5.3-litre V8 to Callaway Engineering in the USA, who helped to develop the engine's four-valve cylinder head. Following a soon-to-end Aston tradition, both the car and the engine were hand-built, the latter carrying a brass plaque listing the name of the mechanic who assembled it.

Initially rated at 330 horsepower, the Virage was soon supplemented by the Virage Vantage with twin superchargers that boosted output to 550 bhp, increasing top speed from 158 mph to 186. Aston also produced a convertible version, the Virage Volante, along with a handful of shooting brakes and even a few custom-built four-door saloons. In total, just over 1,000 cars were made before production ceased in 2000.

"The Virage was the last of a long line of h'Aston Martin GTs stretching back to the DB4. Maybe not as thoroughly h'equipped as FAB 1, but a lovely motor just the same."

47

1990 CHEVROLET CORVETTE ZR-1

The Corvette was supposed to be 'America's sports car', but as the 1990s dawned, even Chevrolet officials had trouble saying that with a straight face. Wall Street wolfs lusted after European metal from Porsche, Lambo and Ferrari, and the only place you'd find a Corvette poster was on a Chevrolet dealer's wall. And then Chevrolet revealed the ZR-1; not at the Detroit Auto Show, but in Geneva. The specs read like a list of hardware that stodgy old General Motors would never contemplate: electronically adjustable dampers, 6-speed manual gearbox and massive ZR-rated Goodyear Gatorback tyres. But most impressive was the engine, an all-aluminium, 32-valve, four-cam V8. The LT5 engine was designed in conjunction with Lotus Engineering and built by boat engine manufacturer Mercury Marine, which had extensive experience building high-performance aluminium engines. Output was 375 horsepower – staggering for the times – and would later rise to 405.

Performance was good enough to generate surprise in Stuttgart and malaise in Maranello: 0–60 in 4.5 seconds, a top speed north of 175 mph and – truly unique for a Corvette, or any American car for that matter – a chassis and suspension that could keep up with the engine. Chevy priced the ZR-1 at $58,995 (c.£38,000), nearly double the cost of a standard Corvette, and early buyers eagerly paid tens of thousands above list price. In one fell swoop, General Motors put themselves on the map as a world-class sports car manufacturer.

This 'ad the gadgets all right, and the horsepower. Jeff Tracy had his eye on one, I reckon, but he can hardly ever get away from command station. (And we're all the safer for it, I say.)"

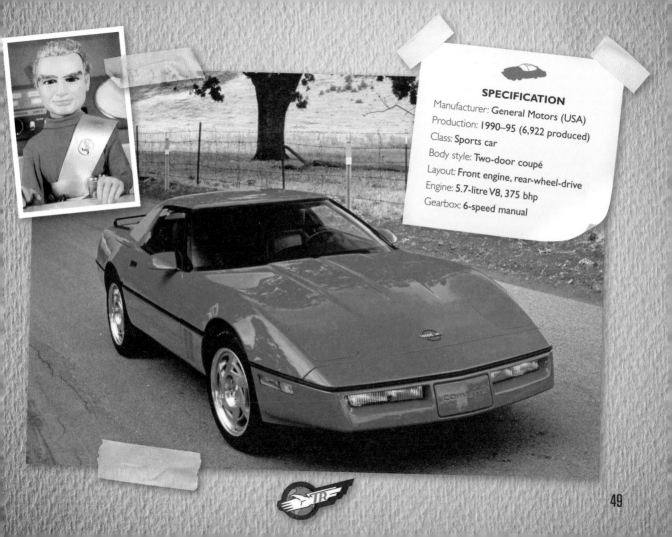

SPECIFICATION

Manufacturer: General Motors (USA)
Production: 1990–95 (6,922 produced)
Class: Sports car
Body style: Two-door coupé
Layout: Front engine, rear-wheel-drive
Engine: 5.7-litre V8, 375 bhp
Gearbox: 6-speed manual

"The Yanks do get some daft ideas into their 'eads, and the turbocharged Syclone pick-up truck was definitely one of them. A truck nearly as fast as a Thunderbird? I'll 'ave one of those, thanks."

1991 GMC SYCLONE

What possessed General Motors to build a pick-up truck that could outrun a Ferrari? Perhaps they were bored with building clones of Chevrolet trucks, or maybe someone slipped some peyote into their coffee. Whatever the reason, GMC started with the compact Sonoma and its industrial-strength 4.3-litre V6 and added a Mitsubishi turbocharger, a Garrett intercooler, and the throttle body and gearbox from a Corvette. Intake, exhaust and engine internals were upgraded to handle 14 psi of boost, and a Borg-Warner transfer case provided full-time all-wheel-drive with a 35/65 front-to-rear power split. Springs, dampers and sway bars were stiffened and the decade-old body was dressed up with a ground effects kit and a jet-black paint job.

The results were unreal: 280 bhp, 350 lb-ft of torque and a claimed 0–60 time of under 5 seconds (the actual figure was closer to 4.5). *Car and Driver* put the Syclone up against a Ferrari 348TS; not only did the Syclone spank it in the quarter mile, but it stopped quicker as well, despite having drum brakes in the rear.

The Syclone was useless as a pick-up truck, its stiff suspension limiting carrying capacity to 227 kg (500 lbs). Still, that doesn't completely explain the slow sales. GM reportedly made just three units for the 1992 model year, as they had not yet sold the 2,995 they built for 1991. 1992 also saw the introduction of an SUV version called the Typhoon; it sold 4,700 copies in its own two-year production run. And then, as suddenly and inexplicably as they appeared, the Syclone and Typhoon were gone and everything went back to normal at GMC. Go figure.

SPECIFICATION

Manufacturer: General Motors (USA)
Production: 1991–92 (2,998 produced)
Class: Sport truck
Body style: Compact pick-up
Layout: Front engine, rear-wheel-drive
Engine: 4.3-litre turbocharged V6, 280 bhp
Gearbox: 4-speed automatic

1992 FORD CROWN VICTORIA POLICE INTERCEPTOR

"I h'am very glad the British bobbies didn't have these when I were on the wrong side of the law. There's no telling where I'd be now. Not making cocktails for Lady Penelope, that's for sure."

Now regarded as one of the best police cars ever made, the Ford Crown Victoria Police Interceptor got off to a slow start. Chrysler and General Motors built what were generally regarded as the best cop cars, but as both companies moved their full-size cars to front-drive platforms, the Ford Crown Victoria was left as America's last rear-drive, body-on-frame sedan – a simple but durable format preferred by American police departments.

Ford took advantage of the situation, spinning off the Police Interceptor into a separate model in 1992 (previously it had been an option package on the Crown Victoria)

and improving its design and durability. Compared to civilian Crown Vics, the Police Interceptors had a beefed-up suspension, greater ground clearance and improved electrical and cooling systems. The 4.6-litre V8 was tuned for up to 250 horsepower, and a choice of rear axle ratios allowed it to reach speeds as high as 130 mph.

By the turn of the millennium, US beat-cops had come to love the Crown Victoria for its roomy interior and the fact that it could drive over a kerb at speed with no ill effects. When Ford announced it would discontinue its rear-drive cars in 2011, police departments across America stockpiled cars and parts. To this day, most American drivers slow to the speed limit when they see a Crown Vic in their rear-view mirror.

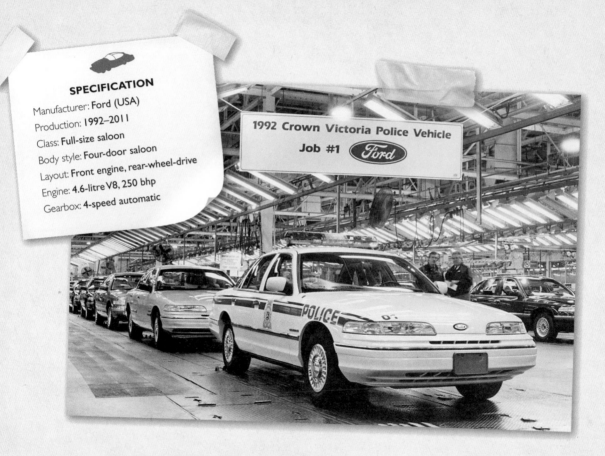

SPECIFICATION

Manufacturer: Ford (USA)

Production: 1992–2011

Class: Full-size saloon

Body style: Four-door saloon

Layout: Front engine, rear-wheel-drive

Engine: 4.6-litre V8, 250 bhp

Gearbox: 4-speed automatic

1992 Crown Victoria Police Vehicle
Job #1 *Ford*

1993 TOYOTA SUPRA TURBO

"The Supra Turbo shows how our Japanese friends don't just make reliable motors – they also know how to go fast. (Just as well we do too, or else we wouldn't 'ave rescued Tin-Tin on that Fireflash flight from Tokyo.)"

SPECIFICATION

Manufacturer: **Toyota (Japan)**

Production: **1993–2002**

Class: **Sports car**

Body style: **Two-door coupé**

Layout: **Front engine, rear-wheel-drive**

Engine: **3.0-litre sequential-turbo inline six, 320 bhp**

Gearbox: **6-speed manual**

By the early 1990s, Toyota had built a reputation for cars that were exceptionally reliable and exceptionally bland, and that made it all the more shocking when the Supra Turbo showed up. Many refer to the Supra as a twin-turbo car, but in fact the Supra's turbochargers were not twins; they were sequential, with a smaller turbocharger that lit up at around 2,500 rpm and a larger one that kicked in at 4,500. On-paper ratings were a heady 320 bhp, 315 lb-ft of torque and a 0–60 time of under 5 seconds, but the 'stepped' nature of the turbos gave the Supra a power curve more like a jet fighter with afterburners. The Supra Turbo even made it into the first *Need for Speed* video game, alongside the Lamborghini Diablo, Dodge Viper and Ferrari 512TR.

The Supra Turbo was one of a crop of Japanese supercars that popped up in the early '90s, including the Honda NSX, Nissan 300 ZX Turbo and Mitsubishi 3000 GT VR4. It was perhaps the only time that young lads lusted after Japanese motors with the same reverence normally reserved for German and Italian cars.

"This speedy Swede is the fastest way to pop down to the shops for yer pipe tobacco and Evenin' Standard. Course I can't do that when we're down at Lady Penelope's mansion, but the open roads more than make up for it."

1994 VOLVO 850 T5-R

By the mid-1990s, Volvo had firmly established itself as a purveyor of sensible, safe motors for the woolly-jumper set. So you can imagine the surprise of the visitors to the 1994 Geneva Motor Show when they walked by the Volvo stand and found this waiting for them. The 850 T5-R was a Volvo unlike anything anyone had ever seen.

It turned out that those big five-spoke wheels, lowered stance, and screaming yellow paint weren't just for show: the 850 T5-R's 2.3-litre, 5-cylinder engine was turbocharged, intercooled, and tuned for 243 bhp and 250 lb-ft of torque. The 850 T5-R ran to 60 mph in just under 6 seconds, this

despite being saddled with a four-speed automatic gearbox, and its cornering agility matched its straight-line speed. The model went on to spur the successful 850R and S/V70R, though neither were as impressive.

SPECIFICATION

Manufacturer: Volvo (Sweden)
Production: 1994 (5,500 produced)
Class: Sport sedan/estate
Body style: Four-door sedan
Layout: Front engine, rear-wheel-drive
Engine: 2.3-litre turbocharged inline 5, 243 bhp
Gearbox: 4-speed automatic

At the same time as the 850 T5-R was introduced, Volvo announced that they would be competing in the British Touring Car Championship with – what else? – an 850 estate. Helmed by ex-Formula 1 drivers Jan Lammers (from Holland) and Rickard Rydell (of Sweden), the BTCC car had a 280 bhp non-turbocharged inline five. It looked mental going around the track and it probably annoyed other racing drivers nearly as much as road-going Volvo estates annoy other road users.

1995 CHRYSLER ATLANTIC CONCEPT

Nowadays, retro-styled cars like the Mini Cooper, Fiat 500, and Dodge Challenger are a common sight on public roads, but it was the Chrysler Atlantic concept car that helped give rise to the retro movement. The story goes that the Atlantic was conceived in a conversation between Chrysler president Bob Lutz and design chief Tom Gale, who were serving as judges at the Pebble Beach Concours d'Elegance. There was a display of concept cars, old and new, and Lutz and Gale decided to build something that would put them all to shame. Lutz made a sketch on a napkin, and upon returning to Michigan, Gale gave his designers the assignment (though not Lutz's sketch) and asked them to come up with their own French-inspired designs.

It was team member Bob Hubbach's creation that ended up forming the basis of the Chrysler Atlantic. The car was clearly inspired by the Bugatti Type 57S Atlantic from which it takes its name; the centre-line crease pays homage to the Bugatti's ventral seam, with teardrop side windows inspired by the Talbot-Lago T150 SS of 1938. The engine was a 4.0-litre inline eight built from a pair of Chrysler Neon engine blocks, and the car was adorned with modern details such as the enormous chrome wheels and neon lighting.

The Atlantic stunned the crowds when it debuted at the 1995 Detroit Auto Show, and while many concept cars are unceremoniously crushed, the Atlantic lives on in a collection at Chrysler's US headquarters.

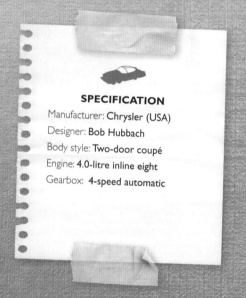

SPECIFICATION
Manufacturer: **Chrysler (USA)**
Designer: **Bob Hubbach**
Body style: **Two-door coupé**
Engine: **4.0-litre inline eight**
Gearbox: **4-speed automatic**

"Now 'ere's a classic like they used to build when I was a nipper. Does me heart proud to see some people still remember what a proper car looks like."

1996 LOTUS ELISE

"I always say that 'success comes with doing what you know best'. (To tell the truth, it was Jeff Tracy who said that, but it's what comes to mind when I look at this beauty of a car. He won't mind.)"

Lotus founder Colin Chapman made his name by building lightweight, minimalist cars (see pages 20–21), but he seemed to turn his back on this idea in the mid-1970s. After his death in 1982, Lotus spent much of its time designing racing and production cars for other people, but in 1996 Lotus returned to Chapman's original vision with the Elise.

With a fibreglass body and lightweight aluminium tub, the Elise weighed 725 kg (1,600 lb) – less than half the mass of a modern-day Ford Mondeo. Fitted with the most modest of engines (in this case, a 118 bhp 1.8-litre Rover K-series) the Elise could get to 60 mph in under six seconds. But on-paper performance does not tell the true story of this car. What made it magical was the way it went down the road (or, more specifically, around the bends). Designed with almost no regard for comfort or convenience, the Elise was a pure driver's machine, one that could grip the asphalt like discarded chewing gum and change direction like a pinball.

The Elise has been offered in a variety of versions and it remains in production to this day (currently with Toyota-sourced power: either a 134 bhp, naturally-aspirated 1.6 or a 217 bhp, supercharged 1.8) along with a coupé version called the Exige. Though crash standards have seen weight increase to 925 kg (2,040 lb), it's a negligible amount, and the driving experience remains true to the original.

SPECIFICATION

Manufacturer: **Lotus (UK)**

Production: **1996–present**

Class: **Sports car**

Body style: **Two-door convertible**

Layout: **Mid-engine, rear-wheel-drive**

Engine: **Various Rover and Toyota engines**

Gearbox: **5- or 6-speed manual**

1997 PLYMOUTH PROWLER

"When Brains was struggling to find a model for Thunderbird 6, he should'a looked here. Classic styling, modern engineering - what more could a Tracy boy want?"

Chrysler first showed the Plymouth Prowler concept in 1993, in a tribute to the street rod (a largely American phenomenon in which an antique car is souped up and heavily modified). No one seriously expected them to put the Prowler into production, and yet that's exactly what they did in 1997. Styled as an homage to the past, the Prowler was actually a rolling test-bed for the future, with extensive use of aluminium in its body, frame and suspension, as well as a magnesium brace under the dash that allowed Chrysler to get some much-needed experience with these lightweight materials.

The public loved the way the Prowler looked, but the press was less enthusiastic about the way it drove. Design and packaging constraints meant the only power-train that would fit was Chrysler's corporate 3.5-litre V6 engine and 4-speed automatic transaxle, neither of which endowed the Prowler with much in the way of sound and fury. Still, the Prowler was successful enough to outlast Plymouth; when Chrysler wound up the 73-year-old brand in 2001, the Prowler was rebranded as a Chrysler and stayed on sale until 2002.

1998 MERCEDES-BENZ CLK-GTR

Designed for the FIA GT Championship series, the Mercedes-Benz CLK-GTR was built around a mid-mounted 6.0-litre V12 engine supported by a carbon fibre-aluminium honeycomb chassis and draped with carbon fibre bodywork that vaguely resembled the CLK coupé from which the car took its name. The CLK-GTR so dominated the 1998 FIA GT Championship GT1 class that no other manufacturer attempted to enter a car for the 1999 season, causing the series to be cancelled.

The road car stayed very close to the racing original; the engine was punched out to 6.9 litres for a power output of 612 bhp, but the 6-speed sequential gearbox was identical to the one in the race car. The car went from 0–60 in 3.8 seconds and had a top speed of 200 mph. This being a Mercedes, the £1 million ($1.5 million) price tag included leather and air conditioning, but luggage space was limited to a couple of small cubbies in the massive door sills, and the sweet song of the V12 was largely drowned out by the whine of the racing gearbox. Mercedes hadn't finished building the production run of CLK-GTRs when the GT1 class was closed down, so they built the bare minimum plus one extra for a total of 26 cars (20 coupés and six roadsters).

"Now 'ere's a road-legal racing car that pulls no punches. It takes nerves of steel to drive one o' these. Luckily me and her ladyship ain't short on that front."

1999 PAGANI ZONDA

"In the right hands – like mine – this 'ere Zonda could take off about as fast as Thunderbird 3, and that's a flippin' rocket! Alan could probably use it as back-up."

It's not unusual for a company to come out of nowhere and take on the Italian exotics, though the resulting cars usually leave a trail of leaking oil, broken electrical bits and plummeting second-hand values. To do it successfully is another thing entirely, and that's what sets the Pagani Zonda apart – that and the fact that Pagani set up shop in Enzo Ferrari's birthplace of Modena, Italy.

Argentinian Horacio Pagani established his career as an engineer for Lamborghini, then started his own company to build carbon-fibre composites for Formula 1 racing cars. In 1992 he formed Pagani Automobili S.p.A. with the intention of creating his own supercar, and seven years later the Zonda C12 made its debut in Geneva, powered by a 389 bhp,

6.0-litre Mercedes V12 that took it to 60 mph in just over 4 seconds. Shortly thereafter, Pagani swapped in Mercedes' 550 bhp 7.0-litre V12, dropping the 0–60 time to 3.5 seconds and upping the top speed to 210 mph. Displacement would rise to 7.3 litres, but the penultimate Zonda, the R, would revert to the 6.0-litre engine – this time with 740 bhp and a 6-speed sequential manual gearbox. The Zonda R made the 0–60 run in as little as 2.6 seconds, and Pagani quoted the top speed as 'over 350 km/h' – that's 217.5 mph.

Pagani wrapped up Zonda production in 2011, replacing the car with the harder-to-pronounce Huayra. And while the Huayra may be faster, it's the Zonda that will be remembered for successfully taking on the Italians.

SPECIFICATION

Manufacturer: **Pagani (Italy)**
Production: **1999–2011 (c.200 produced)**
Class: **Super car**
Body style: **Two-door coupé**
Layout: **Mid engine, rear-wheel-drive**
Engine: **6.0-litre V12, 389 bhp**
Gearbox: **5-speed manual**

2000 BMW Z8

With a thriving business in sports saloons and the successful Z3 roadster already in showrooms, BMW didn't need to build a car like the Z8, and yet build it they did – a handmade, limited-production, ready-made collectible classic that has assumed its expected place in automotive history.

First shown as the Z07 Concept at the 1997 Tokyo Motor Show, the Z8 was an early entrant in the retro-car movement. Its styling paid homage to the US-market 507 roadster of 1956–59, a car whose rarity (just 253 were built) was a consequence of its high price and ponderous handling. The production Z8 looked very similar to the concept, and many people got their first glimpse of the car in the 1999 film *The World Is Not Enough*, in which James Bond's Z8 was unceremoniously cut in half by a giant buzz saw. (That's what he gets for not buying British.)

Like the original 507, the Z8 had a V8 engine, a 400 bhp, 3.9-litre, 32-valve unit borrowed from the M5. Magazine testing put the 0–60 time at 4.5 seconds. Handling expectations were high and most contemporary reports found it intensely satisfying (though *Top Gear's* Jeremy Clarkson famously disagreed, likening its handling to that of a skip lorry). As with the 507, the price was high, at £86,595 (c.$135,000), but this time the punters snapped them up, perhaps realizing that such a lovely and unnecessary endeavour as the Z8 might never be embarked upon again.

SPECIFICATION

Manufacturer: **BMW (Germany)**
Production: **2000–03 (5,703 built)**
Class: **Roadster**
Body style: **Two-door convertible**
Layout: **Front engine, rear-wheel-drive**
Engine: **3.9-litre V8, 400 bhp**
Gearbox: **6-speed manual**

"This would 'ave made a fine motor for that pretend-holiday Lady Penelope and me took on Monte Bianco, France. Provided M'Lady wouldn't have minded sitting up front, that is."

SPECIFICATION

Manufacturer: General Motors (Australia)

Production: 2001–06

Class: Muscle car

Body style: Two-door coupé

Layout: Front engine, rear-wheel-drive

Engine: 5.7-litre V8, 342–402 bhp

Gearbox: 6-speed manual or 4-speed automatic

2001 HOLDEN HSV COUPÉ

"I spent many happy days at her Ladyship's sheep farm in h'Australia, but I would have given me right arm to drive one of these round Bonga Bonga's airstrip."

The Holden Monaro first appeared in the late 1960s as a sport-themed two-door coupé, though it had lost much of its potency by the time General Motors' Australian division killed it off in 1977. The Monaro was reborn in 2001 as a two-door version of the Commodore, and this time the muscle was back, with a choice of a 189 bhp supercharged V6 or a 302 bhp V8. But if you wanted to go *really* fast, the car you wanted was the Holden HSV Coupé, which offered the Monaro's Chevrolet-sourced, 5.7-litre V8, with 342 bhp in the HSV GTO or 402 bhp in the GTS – the latter tuned by US-based Callaway Engineering. The HSV Coupé would later get a 398 bhp, 6.0-litre V8, though its 4.8-second 0–60 run was still a tenth of a second behind the Callaway-tuned 5.7-litre cars). HSV even went on to produce a four-wheel-drive version.

In a rather lovely bit of irony, Australian muscle would make its way to America. After driving the Monaro in Australia, General Motor's North American chairman, Bob Lutz, insisted on importing the car to the USA, where it was sold in 5.7- and 6.0-litre forms as the Pontiac GTO.

2002 FERRARI ENZO

SPECIFICATION

Manufacturer: **Ferrari (Italy)**

Production: **2002–04 (349 produced)**

Class: **Supercar**

Body style: **Two-door coupé**

Layout: **Mid-engine, rear-wheel-drive**

Engine: **6.0-litre V12, 650 bhp**

Gearbox: **6-speed sequential automated manual**

When you're talking about Ferraris, the word 'special' is relative. After all, isn't every Ferrari special? (Well, maybe not the 308.) But the Ferrari Enzo – properly known as the Enzo Ferrari – really is unique, and not just because it bears the founder's name.

As with its predecessor, the F50, the Enzo was inspired by Formula 1, but it wasn't simply a road-legal race car. Not that you would know it from the equipment list: the 6-litre, 650 bhp V12 delivered its power through an F1-style, 6-speed, semi-automatic gearbox, with paddle shifters and lights on the steering wheel to warn of the approaching redline. Steering was racing-car quick, with just 2.2 turns lock-to-lock. The suspension used pushrod-actuated dampers with remote reservoirs, while the brakes used carbon-ceramic discs. And the body? Made of carbon fibre, naturally, as were the seats.

And yet this was a road car, with its rather, erm, unusual styling (courtesy of Pininfarina's Ken Okuyama) and a few concessions to comfort, such as standard-fit air conditioning. Performance was the stuff of dreams: 0–60 in a bit over 3 seconds and a top speed of 218 mph. And if you dreamed of owning one, well, that was just too bad: Ferrari built only 349 examples, and they hand-picked the buyers. Company founder Enzo Ferrari could be a ruthless operator; no question he would have approved.

"The H'Enzo Ferrari is probably the most exclusive car in the world — 'cept for FAB 1, of course."

2003 MITSUBISHI LANCER EVOLUTION VIII

"With nearly 300 turbocharged horsepower, all-wheel-drive and a rock-hard chassis all concealed in a family-saloon wrapper, the H'Evo is the h'ultimate secret weapon (much like 'er Ladyship)."

The Evolution, or 'Evo', was born in 1992 as a street-going version of Mitsubishi's then-new WRC car. Sales were originally limited to Japan, but 'grey market' cars soon started leaking into other countries. Mitsubishi relented and brought the Evolution V to Europe in 1998, but it wasn't until 2003 that the floodgates opened, when the Evo VIII made its way to the USA.

On paper, the Lancer Evolution was a turbocharged, all-wheel-drive performance saloon with a sophisticated set of differentials that gave it superior traction in all driving conditions. In the real world, driving it was like getting a day pass from the laws of physics. The Evo delivered insane amounts of power from its 2-litre engine, while its grip on the pavement defied belief. And its trick all-wheel-drive system made it almost impossible to drive badly: no matter what bone-headed move the driver made, the Evo turned it into more speed.

The Evo was locked in battle with its chief rival, Subaru's Impreza WRX STI. And while fans of both brands will argue for generations to come, most agree that the Subaru was more civilized, while the Lancer was more raw. The Evo's interior was dreadful, the ride was punishing and the noise was unbearable, but for drivers who had nerves of steel and vertebrae of granite, few cars could thrill as the Evo did.

SPECIFICATION

Manufacturer: **Mitsubishi (Japan)**
Production: **2003–05**
Class: **Sports sedan**
Body style: **Four-door saloon**
Layout: **Front engine, all-wheel-drive**
Engine: **2.0-litre turbocharged, 276 bhp**
Gearbox: **5- or 6-speed manual**

2004 PORSCHE CARRERA GT

"Some people say the Carrera GT is one of the most frightening cars h'ever made. But after the time I let one of me nephews drive FAB 1, I don't think anything could frighten me ever again."

The Carrera GT was built purely as a street car, albeit one that was about as close to a racing machine as was possible. The spec sheet certainly read like something from Formula 1: carbon fibre for the monocoque chassis, bodywork and seats; ceramic composite brakes and clutch; and a double-wishbone suspension with inboard-mounted springs and dampers. And the engine – oh, the engine! – was a 605 bhp, 5.7-litre V10 with titanium connecting rods, aluminium pistons and a dry-sump oiling system. Instead of a fancy F1-style flappy-paddle gearbox, the Carrera had a traditional 6-speed manual. (How better to show off Porsche's new dual-disc ceramic composite clutch?) Among the few reminders that this was a road car rather than a race car: air con, sat nav, a Bose stereo and a removable roof.

Car and Driver magazine reported a 0–60 time of 3.3 seconds, and the factory claimed a top speed of 205 mph. The Carrera GT quickly developed a reputation for tricky at-the-limit handling, especially after US actor Paul Walker died while being one of its passengers. In truth, the Carrera GT was a car that demanded respect – just like a racing car.

2005 HOLDEN EFIJY

Street rods are a largely American phenomenon, but the Australians showed the world they know how it's done with the 2005 Holden Efijy concept. Conceived by Holden chief designer Richard Ferlazzo, the Efijy was built to celebrate the 50th anniversary of Holden's iconic FJ. The fibreglass body exhibited the classic 'chopped and channelled' look in which the roof is lowered and the body is remounted lower on the floor. Details were a mix of modern and classic, with massive aluminium billet wheels and a retro-themed, touch-screen control system. And the Efijy wasn't just a styling study; built on a Chevrolet Corvette chassis, it was a fully operable car powered by a 6.0-litre supercharged V8. At the 2007 Detroit Auto Show, it was named Concept Car of the Year, and in the USA it is seen as one of the greatest street rods ever created.

"When I first saw this car, I felt like I'd taken a whiff of that cutting gas Brains once came up with. Just about knocked me right h'over."

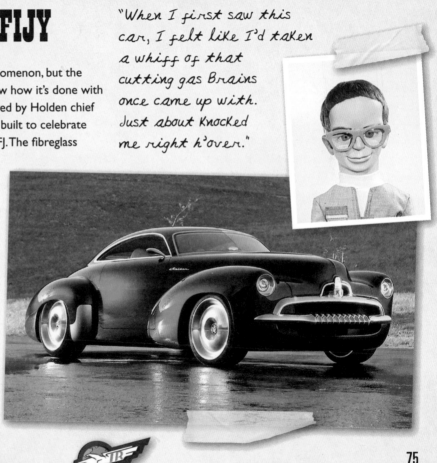

2006 KOENIGSEGG CCX

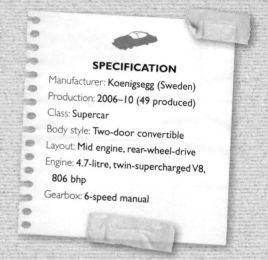

SPECIFICATION
Manufacturer: Koenigsegg (Sweden)
Production: 2006–10 (49 produced)
Class: Supercar
Body style: Two-door convertible
Layout: Mid engine, rear-wheel-drive
Engine: 4.7-litre, twin-supercharged V8,
   806 bhp
Gearbox: 6-speed manual

'Swedish cars are synonymous with safety.' That phrase has been written more times than anyone can count and one has to imagine that the Swedes were bound to get sick of it after a while. While Volvo and Saab were sold off to the Chinese (perhaps in an attempt to get the world to start saying 'Chinese cars are synonymous with safety'?) one Swede, a certain Christian von Koenigsegg, decided to take a more radical approach.

Von Koenigsegg set out to design a supercar that could match the performance of the McLaren F1, including its 240 mph top speed. His first effort, the Ford-powered 655 bhp CC8S, did exactly that, but von Koenigsegg wanted more – he wanted a hypercar that would rule the world, which meant it would have to be legal and useable planet-wide. And so he created the CCX, designed to meet America's tough crash and emissions standards, and to run on its less-than-brilliant 95-octane petrol.

This time, Koenigsegg used a home-grown engine: a 4.7-litre twin-supercharged V8 that produced 806 bhp on American fuel. (The CCXR version could make 1,018 bhp when run on ethanol.) Low weight, low drag, and that epic V8 gave it a 0–60 time of 3.1 seconds and a top speed of a ridiculous 250 mph. What about safety? Well, it did have a couple of airbags, but there was no traction or stability control, and adjustable dampers allowed the driver to fine-tune the handling balance. The CCX was designed for advanced-level drivers and would happily bite those of lesser skills square in the arse. The Swedish may still be known more for safe cars than supercars, but thanks to the Koenigsegg CCX, that might someday change.

"I remember the Duchess worrying about her old Portrait of a Gazelle by Bricasso. I'd 'ave put me money in a real work of art, like this."

2007 ALFA ROMEO 8C COMPETIZIONE

"H'Italy is a land of beauty – beautiful art and architecture, beautiful women, an' beautiful cars like this here H'Alfa Romeo."

A good Alfa Romeo is like a supermodel: beautiful, passionate, temperamental and difficult to live with. (A bad Alfa Romeo, on the other hand, is more like a rebadged Fiat.) The 8C Competizione was an attempt to bring back the best of Alfa, and by and large, it did.

The 8C Competizione was styled to recall an alphanumeric soup of classic Alfas from the 1940s and '50s and link them to Alfa's modern-day cars. It was a delicate mission that designer Wolfgang Egger pulled off rather well.

Looking at the 8C Competizione, it was possible to forget that it was a mere mode of transportation, and regard it purely as a thing of beauty. But its engineering was just as attractive. Thanks to the incestuous relationship between Fiat's divisions, the 8C borrowed its basic substructure from Maserati, who also assembled the car, though the engine – Maserati's 4.7-litre V8 – was actually put together by Ferrari. In keeping with Alfa tradition, the gearbox was at the rear of the car, though it was shifted Maranello-style with paddle shifters on the steering wheel. Though the 8C was fast (0-60 in 4.2 seconds, top speed 182 mph), road manners were not quite up to Ferrari or Lambo standards. Since only 500 were made, not many people had the opportunity to find out.

SPECIFICATION

Manufacturer: Alfa Romeo (Italy)

Production: 2007–09 (500 produced)

Class: Sports car

Body style: Two-door coupé

Layout: Front engine, rear-wheel-drive

Engine: 4.7-litre V8, 444 bhp

Gearbox: 6-speed semi-automatic

2008 DODGE CHALLENGER SRT8

"Those Americans do love their big cars and their big h'engines. It's nice to see a yank tank that can do more than go in a straight line."

The muscle car is a quintessentially American creation: a ridiculously large and powerful engine paired with a rudimentary suspension and primitive brakes, all held together by massive stick-on tape stripes. These were the dinosaurs that roamed the streets of the USA throughout the 1960s and early 70s, until stricter emissions and increasing petrol prices led to their extinction.

And then, in 2008, one of the dinosaurs came back to life. It was the Dodge Challenger, and what stunned American 'gearheads' was not just the 6.1-litre V8 under the bonnet, but the fact that it bore such a strong resemblance to the original 1970 Challenger – a feat all the more amazing when you consider that the car was based on the big Chrysler 300 saloon. Horsepower was 425, a magic number among muscle car fans, as that was the advertised output of Chrysler's legendary 426 HEMI V8. The new Challenger certainly played the part of a muscle car; it was very loud and very quick, running to 60 mph in 4.7 seconds. Handling was not as bad as the 1970 original, though the old Mercedes bones from which Chrysler's LX platform was built hardly qualified it as a sporting ride. But the Challenger had the presence and the pace of a proper muscle car, and that was all the Americans needed to fall in love with it.

SPECIFICATION

Manufacturer: **Chrysler (USA)**
Production: **2008–present**
Class: **Muscle car**
Body style: **Two-door coupé**
Layout: **Front engine, rear-wheel-drive**
Engine: **6.1-litre V8, 425 bhp**
Gearbox: **4-speed automatic**

2009 NISSAN GT-R

"This car puts me in the mind of when Alan got back into the racing business. With Brains as his mechanic, I bet he could have run one 'eck of a race in this."

SPECIFICATION

Manufacturer: Nissan (Japan)

Production: 2007–present

Class: Sports car

Body style: Two-door coupé

Layout: Front engine, all-wheel-drive

Engine: 3.8-litre twin-turbocharged V6, 480 bhp

Gearbox: 6-speed dual clutch

For many petrolheads, it is the mechanical nature of the automobile that makes it a thing of beauty: the interaction of cogs and pistons, valves and clutches, steel and oil that work together to turn petrol into forward motion.

People who feel that way should *not* drive a Nissan GT-R.

First introduced in Japan in 2007, the GT-R stormed onto the world scene in 2009 as a harbinger of our computerized future. With its 480 horsepower, twin-turbo V6, rear-mounted dual-clutch gearbox, and electronic all-wheel-drive system, the GT-R achieved things that Messrs. Rolls and Royce never could have achieved with the Edwardian technology available to them. While the driver moved the pedals and the steering wheel, it was the computers that did the split-second calculations, optimizing power production and delivery to take advantage of every last bit of traction available.

Many critics complained that the GT-R was far too computerized, as it relegated driver skill (or lack thereof) to a peripheral concern. But they agreed that it was blindingly quick – not only could it jump to 60 mph in 3.5 seconds, but it could tear up a racetrack like Godzilla attacking a Tokyo high-rise.

2010 BUGATTI VEYRON 16.4 SUPER SPORT

When it was first introduced in the fall of 2005, the Bugatti Veyron was a car of superlatives, with a 1,001 horsepower engine, a 250 mph top speed and a €1.6 million price tag (that's around $1.2 million or £800,000, for those that are counting). Could a car get any better? It did in 2010, when Bugatti introduced the Veyron 16.4 Super Sport.

With five years of experience, Bugatti's engineers knew where improvements could be made. They cleaned up the aerodynamics, going so far as to eliminate the two signature roof scoops and replacing them with aircraft-style ducts that formed a tunnel over the 16-cylinder engine.

The body structure and suspension were modified to increase torsional rigidity and sharpen the Veyron's responses, while the aerodynamics were tweaked to increase downforce. Upping the power was a simple matter of enlarging the engine's four turbochargers and their intercoolers, which bumped the output to 1,200 horsepower and 1,106 lb-ft of torque. The time from 0–60 with launch mode engaged was 2.5 seconds,

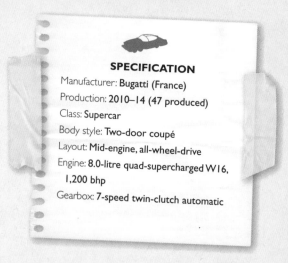

SPECIFICATION

Manufacturer: **Bugatti (France)**
Production: **2010–14 (47 produced)**
Class: **Supercar**
Body style: **Two-door coupé**
Layout: **Mid-engine, all-wheel-drive**
Engine: **8.0-litre quad-supercharged W16, 1,200 bhp**
Gearbox: **7-speed twin-clutch automatic**

and while the Super Sport was able to reach nearly 268 mph on the track, production models (except the limited-run World Record Edition, pictured right) were limited to 258 mph to preserve the tyres, four of which cost as much as a BMW 3-Series. And the price? A cool €1,650,000, ensuring that the mere 47 Super Sports produced would remain as exclusive as they were exquisite.

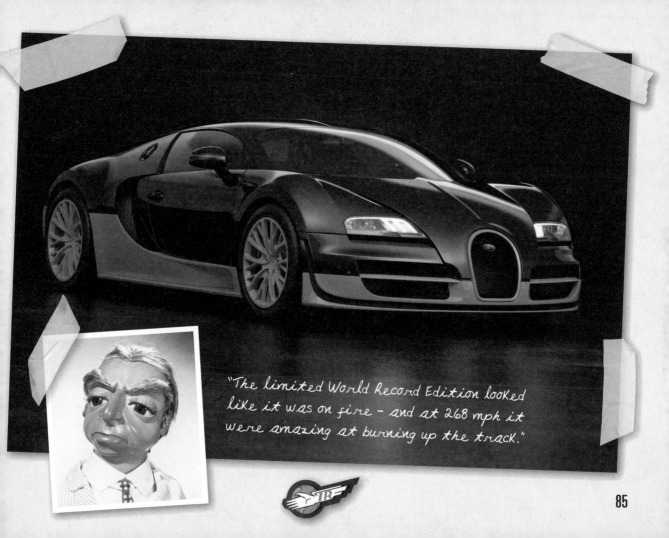

"The limited World Record Edition looked like it was on fire – and at 268 mph it were amazing at burning up the track."

2011 LAMBORGHINI AVENTADOR

When you're Lamborghini, it's rather tough to follow your own act. Making things more difficult for the Aventador was the fact that it was the new top-of-the-range Lambo.

Wide and flat like its predecessors, the Aventador's styling echoed the sharp creases and severe angles of the limited-run Reventon, itself inspired by the F-117 Nighthawk stealth fighter. Under the bonnet, it stayed true to big-Lambo tradition: while other supercars were turning to turbochargers and hybrid drivetrains, Lamborghini fitted a naturally aspirated V12. The engine pulled 691 bhp from its 6.5-litre displacement, which was enough to drive the Aventador to 60 mph in 2.9 seconds and on to 217 mph. The gearbox was also all-new: a 7-speed, single-clutch, semi-automated manual. Like all full-size Lamborghinis going back to the 1993 Diablo VT, the Aventador employed all-wheel-drive. The technology under the bodywork was state-of-the-art: a carbon-fibre monocoque chassis, pushrod suspension, carbon-ceramic brakes and a video-screen instrument panel. And the soul was that of a classic supercar, which is just how a Lambo ought to be.

"I wonder if the Aventador's stealth-fighter styling would help keep H' International Rescue from being photographed by that mad hooded bloke?"

2012 TESLA MODEL S

"Brains has taken to talking about these here electric cars like they're something special. Don't tell 'im, but this one really is."

For most petrolheads, the prospect of the electric car is pretty dreary, or at least it was until Tesla came along. The Model S was a full-size luxury car with a shape that echoed the contemporary Audi A7 and Jaguar XJ, but instead of an engine under its long bonnet, it had a second boot. The electric motor was in the rear and it produced either 302 or 416 bhp, with 0–60 times ranging from 5.9 seconds for the least-expensive model down to 4.2 for the P85 performance version (this would later drop to 3.2 seconds in the all-wheel-drive P85D). And while most electric cars were delivering around 80 miles per charge, the Model S returned between 208 and 295 miles, depending on which battery was fitted. A 480-volt fast-charge system could add 200 miles' worth of juice in 30 minutes, and Tesla built a Supercharger network that allowed the Model S to be driven from Sweden to Spain or Seattle to Sarasota. So there was no longer a feasible excuse to guzzle gas.

The Model S racked up enough Car of the Year accolades to fill its front boot, and quickly became a runaway success. Suddenly the electric future began to look a lot less grim.

2013 ROLLS-ROYCE FAB 1

"It's nice to see a modern-day FAB 1, although I don't know as I'd want to drive Lady Penelope around without my concealed harpoon guns."

SPECIFICATION

Manufacturer: **Rolls-Royce (UK)**

Production: **2013 (1 produced)**

Class: **Luxury car**

Body style: **Four-door saloon**

Layout: **Front engine, rear-wheel-drive**

Engine: **6.6-litre twin-turbocharged V12, 563 bhp**

Gearbox: **8-speed automatic**

The world has never seen anything quite like Lady Penelope's fabulous FAB 1, but in 2013 Rolls-Royce created a pink-and-silver extended-wheelbase Ghost as an homage to the original. And the new FAB 1 had a rescue mission of its own: it was designed to raise money for Breast Cancer Care, a UK-based charity.

Along with the pink colour scheme (essential!), the cabin was done up for Lady Penelope's comfort: pink and crème upholstery, hand-embroidered headrests with a pink ribbon logo, a champagne chiller, hand-finished wood tables, and pink umbrellas concealed in the doors. And should her Ladyship find herself in a particular hurry, FAB 1 had a 6.6-litre, twin-turbocharged V12 under the silver-satin bonnet, with enough power to accelerate the car to 60 mph in 5 seconds and on to an electronically limited top speed of 155 mph.

FAB 1 started her rescue work for Breast Cancer Care right away, with a journey from Land's End, Cornwall, to John O'Groats, Scotland. The car then embarked on a year-long fund-raising assignment, in which supporters were invited to hire the car (complete with chauffeur, albeit sadly not Parker).

SPECIFICATION

Manufacturer: **McLaren (UK)**
Production: **2014–present**
Class: **Supercar**
Body style: **Two-door coupé**
Layout: **Mid-engine, rear-wheel-drive**
Engine: **3.8-litre twin-turbocharged V8/ electric motor, 903 bhp**
Gearbox: **7-speed dual clutch**

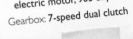

2014 McLaREN P1

"Nine hundred an' three horsepower? I bet H'Alan Tracy could'a used that h'extra power the time he and Thunderbird 3 nearly got themselves dragged into the flipping sun!"

If you say 'plug-in hybrid', most people think of a fuel-sipping green-mobile like the Toyota Prius. So when McLaren introduced their take on the plug-in hybrid, it wasn't exactly what most people were expecting.

The P1's hybrid power-train was built around a 3.8-litre, twin-turbocharged V8 and an electric motor, which worked together to produce a staggering 903 bhp. Left in automatic mode, the P1 employed the electric motor's 'torque fill' function, which would fill in the gaps in the petrol engine's power delivery, such as when the dual-clutch gearbox was changing gears. The driver could also activate the electric motor manually with a steering-wheel-mounted boost button. 0-60 came up in 2.7 seconds, and the P1 would reach 217 mph before the computers prevented it from going any faster. And if the neighbours complained about the harm the P1 was doing to the environment, all the driver had to do was switch it to electric mode and pop down to the shops on battery power.

Trick power-train aside, the P1 was a proper supercar, with an electronic hydro-pneumatic suspension, active aerodynamics, bespoke Pirelli tires, carbon-ceramic brakes powerful enough to stop time, and enough carbon fibre to… well, to build a proper supercar. No surprise that the entire production run of 375 P1s sold out within a few weeks. After all, it was clearly a better choice than a plug-in Prius.

2015 JAGUAR F-TYPE

"The E-Type is a 1960s British classic, and as we well know, everything what's good lasts. And so 'ere it is again, in 2015. Just like the Thunderbirds."

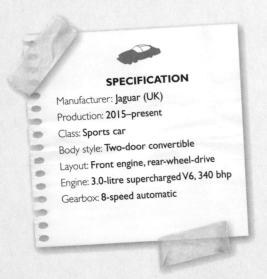

SPECIFICATION

Manufacturer: **Jaguar (UK)**

Production: **2015–present**

Class: **Sports car**

Body style: **Two-door convertible**

Layout: **Front engine, rear-wheel-drive**

Engine: **3.0-litre supercharged V6, 340 bhp**

Gearbox: **8-speed automatic**

The 1961 Jaguar E-Type is regarded as one of the world's greatest sports cars, and all through the ups and downs that Jaguar has endured in the decades since, car enthusiasts have been awaiting its return. Their patience was rewarded in 2015, when Jaguar introduced the F-Type, the spiritual successor to the much-vaunted E-Type Jag.

And a proper successor it was. With a more subtle interpretation of the E's long-bonnet, short-boot body, the F-Type was both beautiful and understated – all the more so once you realized what was under the sheet metal. Power came from a supercharged V6 delivering 340 bhp in the base model and 380 bhp in the S, while the F-Type R packed a 495 bhp supercharged V8. Both engines had an exhaust note guaranteed to thrill the driver and scare the horses.

But big power was nothing new to Jaguar; what set the F-Type apart was its sublime chassis, one that refused to be overwhelmed by all that power. Out on the track, the F-Type was all business, a machine designed purely to turn intention into speed. That it could be so civilized yet so animalistic is what made the F-Type a great sports car, and a true heir to the E-Type's throne.

INDEX

ACKNOWLEDGMENTS

Author Acknowledgments

Thanks to Robin, Andrew and Robert for their ever-present love and support; to Jeff Zurschmeide for his help with car selection; to Sarah Tomley and Tracy Killick for their patience and guidance; and to Parker, into whose head it was so enjoyable to (figuratively) climb. No one asked me if I wanted to dedicate this book to anyone, but if they did, it'd be my father, Toby Gold. Dad, thanks for encouraging me and telling me how proud of me you were, and I'm pleased that my name will be on your bookshelf written in something other than crayon.

Picture Credits

Alamy AF archive 44; eVox/Drive Images 82 (main), 83; Goddard Automotive 62; Achim Hartmann/culture-images GmbH 65 left, 65 right; Motoring Picture Library (21 main), 61, 78 (main); Tim Peeler 17; Fluger Rene/CTK 86 below; Hans Dieter Seufert/culture-images GmbH 35 (main), 71 (main); Phil Talbot 40 below; Chris Wilson 10 below; Tom Wood 15 (main), 22 (main); WENN Ltd. 75 (main). © **all rights reserved by the Colt Car Company Limited** 72. **Bentley Motors Limited** 41. **BMW Group** 29 above. **Bugatti** 85. **By kind permission of the Centro Storico Fiat** 81 (main). **Corbis** Car Culture 11; David Freers/Transtock 81 (main); Transtock 55 (main). **Courtesy of Ford Images** 53. **Daimler AG** 63 below. **Dreamstime** Jason Schulz 31 (main). **FCA US LLC** 12 above, 12 below, 59(main). **Getty Images** Eamonn M. McCormack 89 (main). **General Motors** 36 left, 46 (main), 50 (main). **Holden Special Vehicles** 68. **Jaguar UK** 93 (main). **Kenosha News image by Kevin Poirier** 28. **Koenigsegg Automotive AB** 77 left, 77 above right. **McLaren Automotive** 90 above, 90 (main). **Photo courtesy Barrett-Jackson Auction Co., LLC.** 9 (main). **Porsche AG** 24, 25, 74. **Renault** 33. **Rex Features** Magic Cars Pics 26 (main), 38 (main), 43 (main), 47, 49 (main). **Shutterstock** Teddy Leung 87. **Volvo Cars** 56 (main).

Credits

Editorial Director: Trevor Davies
Production Controller: Sarah-Jayne Johnson

Produced for Octopus Publishing Group Ltd by Tracy Killick Art Direction and Design and www.editorsonline.org
Art Director: Tracy Killick
Commissioning Editor: Sarah Tomley
Indexer: Hilary Bird